curious about

SADDLE BRONC RIDING

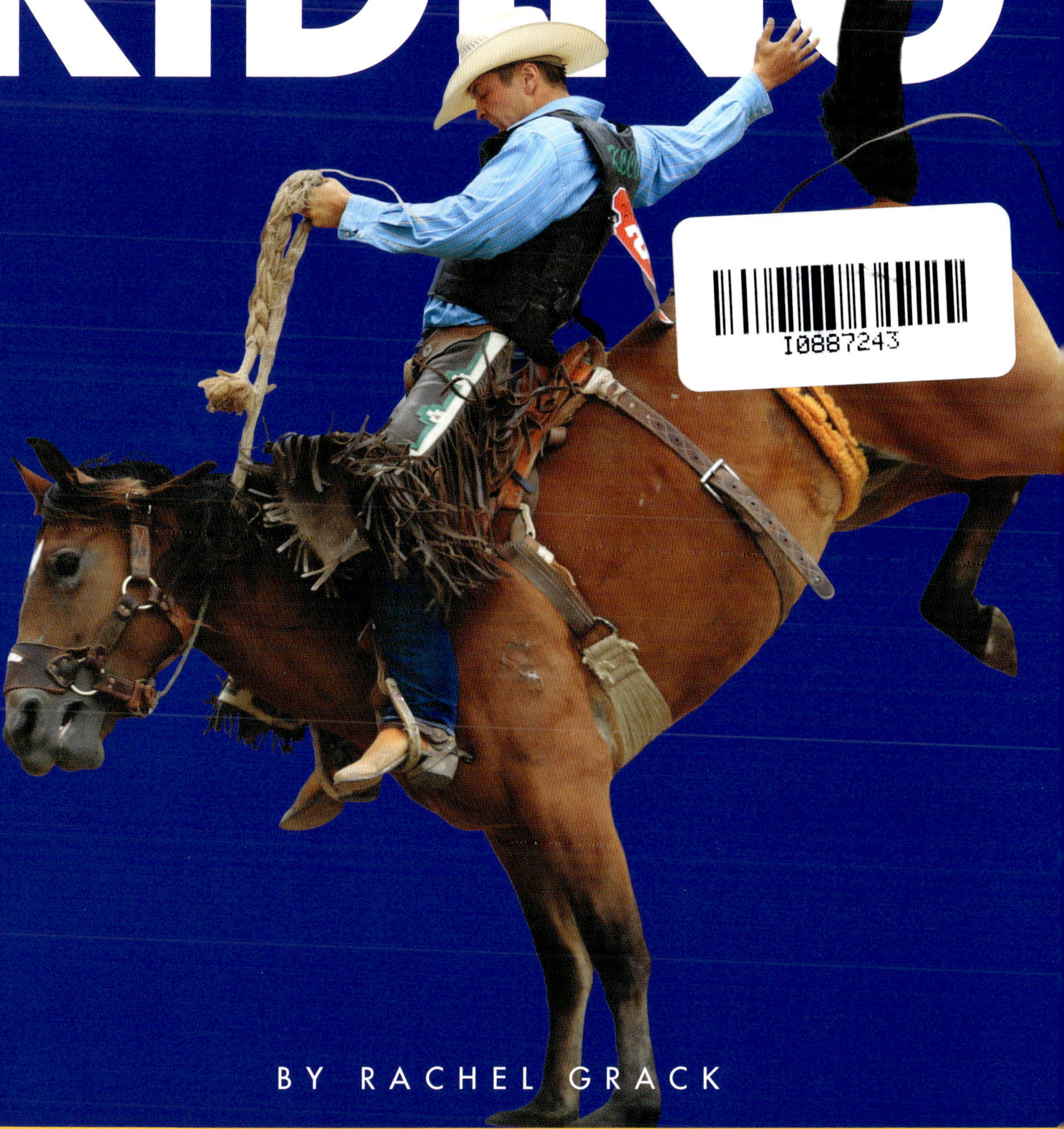

BY RACHEL GRACK

AMICUS LEARNING

I0887243

What are you

curious about?

3

CHAPTER THREE

Bringing Home the Win

PAGE
18

Curious About is published by
Amicus Learning, an imprint of Amicus
P.O. Box 227, Mankato, MN 56002
www.amicuspublishing.us

Copyright © 2025 Amicus.
International copyright reserved in all countries.
No part of this book may be reproduced in any
form without written permission from the publisher.

Editors: Ana Brauer and Megan Siewert
Series Designer: Kathleen Petelinsek
Book Designer and Photo Researcher: Kathleen Petelinsek

Library of Congress Cataloging-in-Publication Data
Names: Koestler-Grack, Rachel A., 1973– author.
Title: Curious about saddle bronc riding / by Rachel Grack.
Description: Mankato, MN : Curious About is published by Amicus Learning, [2025] | Series: Curious about Rodeo | Includes bibliographical references and index. | Audience: Ages 6–9 years | Audience: Grades 2–3 | Summary: "Learn how cowboys and cowgirls compete in saddle bronc riding rodeo events in this question-and-answer book for elementary-aged readers. Includes infographics and back matter to support research skills along with table of contents, glossary, books and websites for further research, and index"— Provided by publisher.
Identifiers: LCCN 2024015010 (print) | LCCN 2024015011 (ebook) | ISBN 9798892000871 (lib bdg) | ISBN 9798892001458 (paperback) | ISBN 9798892002035 (ebook)
Subjects: LCSH: Bronc riding—Juvenile literature.
Classification: LCC GV1834.45.B75 K645 2025 (print) | LCC GV1834.45.B75 (ebook) | DDC 791.8/4—dc23/eng/20240508
LC record available at https://lccn.loc.gov/2024015010
LC ebook record available at https://lccn.loc.gov/2024015011

Photo Credits: Alamy Stock Photo/Brigette Supernova, 3, 20–21, H. Mark Weidman Photography, 9, Robert McGouey, 2, 15, Xinhua, cover, 1; Dreamstime/Michael Turner, 5, Michele Jackson, 2, 7, 10–11; Shutterstock/Callipso88, 6, Gwoeii, 19, Kilroy79, 19, KK Stock, 19, Kobby Dagan, 16–17, Margo Harrison, 12–13, Olga_i, 6, patti jean_images & designs by patti jean, 8, Svetsol, 19, zooco, 19

Printed in China

CHAPTER ONE

What is saddle bronc riding?

It's a rodeo sport. Riders try to stay on a bucking horse for eight seconds. Cowboys saddle up the bronc in the **chute**. The rider climbs on and takes the reins with one hand. He nods and the gate swings open. The bronc bursts out jumping and kicking wildly. Can he hold on?

DID YOU KNOW?
Most professional saddle bronc riders are men. Women's ranch bronc riding is becoming more popular, though.

The horse takes off running as soon as the chute gate opens.

What are broncs?

WHAT MAKES A SADDLE BRONC BRED TO BUCK?

	Coldblood Draft Horse		Hotblood High-energy Breeds
Breed	Belgian, Clydesdale	+	Thoroughbred, Arabian
Traits	Quiet, Calm, Heavy-bodied		Nervous, Lively, Light, Quick

They are untrained horses. They are **bred** to buck. Many saddle broncs are part **draft horse**. Their strong, heavy bodies deliver sturdy kicks. They are crossed with high-energy breeds. This makes saddle broncs the perfect mix of powerful and feisty.

DID YOU KNOW?
Saddle bronc riding is a roughstock event. Roughstock are the bucking horses and bulls used at rodeos.

Warmblood Bronc

Roughstock

Powerful and Feisty

CHAPTER TWO

Why are the rider's feet up?

He's marking out the horse. This happens as the chute opens. The rider leans back and stretches out his legs. Both **spurs** touch the horse above its shoulders. He must hold his boot heels steady for the bronc's first jump. The bronc leaps into the ring. Its front legs hit the dirt. The rider marked out! Then he begins spurring.

Cowboy spurs

Some riders wear mouth guards to protect their jaws and teeth.

What is spurring?

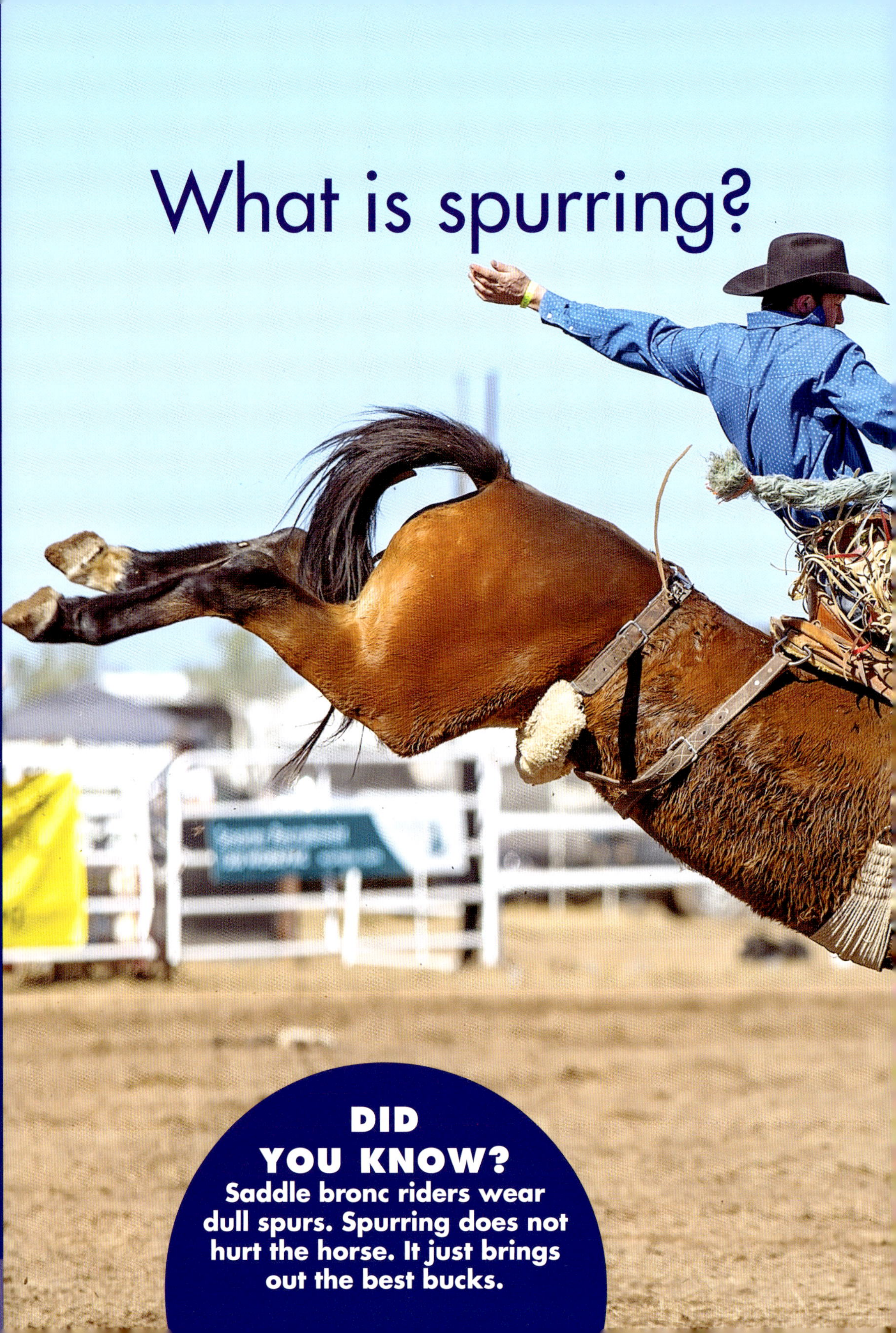

DID YOU KNOW?
Saddle bronc riders wear dull spurs. Spurring does not hurt the horse. It just brings out the best bucks.

That's when the rider rolls his spurs across the horse. Spurring leads to stronger bucks. He keeps his toes pointed out. He rolls his spurs from the shoulders to the back of the saddle. He kicks his heels back up to the neck. He spurs again while the horse keeps bucking.

Riders are only allowed to use one hand during their ride.

How do riders stay on?

SADDLE BRONC RIDING GEAR

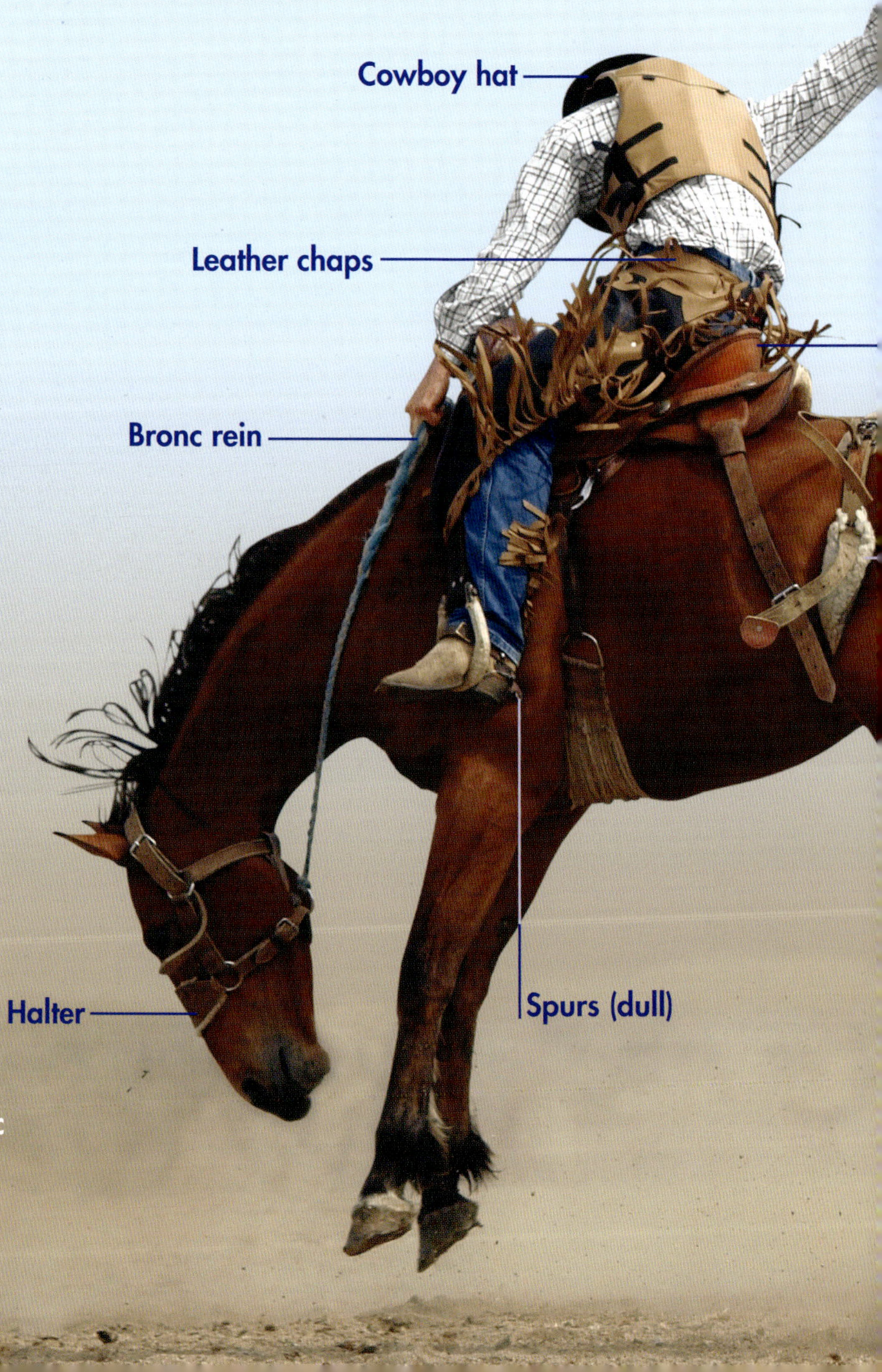

A good bronc saddle helps the rider stay in the seat.

It takes strength, skill, and practice. Riders hold on to the bronc rein. The way they grip the rope matters. A higher grip makes the rein looser. That's too much slack. The rider could be bucked off! Riders must get into **rhythm** with the bronc's bucks. This is probably the trickiest part.

DID YOU KNOW?
Saddle broncs love to buck. No one makes them. But the fleece-lined flank strap gets them to have stronger bucks.

A bronc bucks with rhythm?

Yes! Each bronc has a bucking style. Riders try to match that style. They move their bodies with the bucking horse. It kind of looks like dancing! Both the bronc and the rider get judged on style. Riders must time their rhythm with their spurring action. It's a lot to master in eight seconds!

DID YOU KNOW?
Riders keep their chins down and eyes on the horse's shoulders. This helps them with rhythm and timing.

It takes a lot of time and practice to ride a bronc.

Pickup riders usually work in pairs. They keep riders and horses safe.

What happens when riders get bucked off?

It gets dangerous. They could get kicked or stomped on. Pickup riders rush to the rescue! These heroes on horseback protect riders on the ground. They herd the broncs safely away. Riders sometimes get stuck in the **stirrups**. Pickup riders help them dismount.

What is a no score?

Uh-oh. The rider got bucked off or broke a rule. Maybe he failed to mark out the horse. Perhaps his foot slipped out of the stirrup. The rest of his ride does not count. Riders often have more than one chance to ride. Maybe next **go-round**!

DID YOU KNOW?
Riders cannot use their free hand to touch the horse, saddle, or rein.

"NO SCORE" RULES

1. FAIL TO MARK OUT HORSE

2. TOUCH THE HORSE, SADDLE, OR REIN WITH FREE HAND

3. CHANGE HANDS ON REIN

4. FOOT SLIPS OUT OF STIRRUP

5. BUCKED OFF

How do riders get scored?

SADDLE BRONC SCORING

	HORSE: 1–25
JUDGE 1	23/25
JUDGE 2	22/25
SCORE	45

Two judges score the event. The eight-second buzzer sounds. The rider made it! Judges rate the bronc's kicks and twists. Were they high and strong? Judges watch the rider's spurring action, style, and rhythm. Toes pointed out with long spurring strokes score higher. Anything over 80 is a good ride!

Rodeos have several staff members who keep track of the scores and the riders.

RIDER: 1–25		POSSIBLE POINTS: 100
20/25		43/50
21/25		43/50
41		86/100

STAY CURIOUS

ASK MORE QUESTIONS

Who is the best saddle bronc rider?

How many go-rounds are there?

Try a BIG QUESTION: How much practice does saddle bronc riding take?

SEARCH FOR ANSWERS

Search the library catalog or the Internet.
A librarian, teacher, or parent can help you.

Using Keywords
Find the looking glass.

Keywords are the most important words in your question.

If you want to know:

- who holds the world record in saddle bronc riding, type: BEST SADDLE BRONC RIDERS
- more about go-rounds, type: RODEO GO-ROUNDS

LEARN MORE

FIND GOOD SOURCES

Here are some good, safe sources you can use in your research.
Your librarian can help you find more.

Books

Bareback Riding
by Rachel Grack, 2025.

Bull Riding
by Heather Kissock, 2021.

Internet Sites

Britannica Kids: Rodeos
https://www.britannica.com/sports/saddle-bronc-riding
Britannica is an encyclopedia with educational information on many topics. Learn more about rodeos and saddle bronc riding.

Kiddle: Rodeo
https://kids.kiddle.co/Rodeo
Kiddle is an online encyclopedia for kids. Search for information on a wide variety of educational topics.

Every effort has been made to ensure that these websites are appropriate for children. However, because of the nature of the Internet, it is impossible to guarantee that these sites will remain active indefinitely or that their contents will not be altered.

SHARE AND TAKE ACTION

Watch saddle bronc riding.
Ask an adult to help you find videos.

Take a horseback riding class.
Learn how to ride a trained horse and see if you like riding.

Attend a rodeo.
See the horse's rhythm firsthand!

GLOSSARY

bred When animals are mated together to produce certain characteristics.

chute A pen that holds animals in position so rider can safely mount.

draft horse A tall, powerful horse that is bred to pull carts and equipment.

go-round Each round of rodeo competitions; many rodeos have more than one round.

rhythm A movement in which an action repeats regularly.

spurs The spiked wheels on the heel of a rider's boots.

stirrup The part of a saddle that holds a rider's foot while riding.

INDEX

About the Author

Rachel Grack has been writing children's nonfiction for twenty-five years. She lives on a ranch in the heart of rodeo country (southern Arizona). Some evenings, she wanders over to watch her neighbors in friendly roping competitions. A western restaurant in town offers weekly bull riding and mutton busting. But Rachel much prefers a quiet ride on her gentle paint horse, Lady.